Getting Your ADHD Child to the Aha! Moment: Effective School & Homework Strategies

Sharlene Alexander

ISBN: 146091144X
ISBN-13: 978-1460911440

DEDICATION

This book is dedicated to the parents who work hard and push for the best for their children, among those parents is my own mother.

CONTENTS

AUTHOR'S NOTE

The inspiration and suggestions in the book have actually been applied to children in the classroom and in the home. This book brings together research from top professionals in the fields of medicine, child psychiatry, and education. The key to homework success is patience and consistency. I encourage all parents to continue to stay positive even under challenging circumstances. I have seen true successes when parents are consistent and provide the necessary support and structure. My hope is that this book will answer your questions and provide solutions to help your child succeed.

Get resources at: www.mommyalertadhd.com

1 READING

READING SKILLS

- **Remember in the beginning, it doesn't matter what your child is reading, it matters that they are reading.** Your child can read the lyrics to his favorite songs, comic books, or books with pictures. Bookstore employees or librarians can help your child pick out a great book.
- **The reading can be overwhelming.** Your child can read one word and you read the next, alternating back and forth.
- **Practice pronunciation.** Visually show your child how you form each word with your mouth.
- **Show child this model to emphasize reading from left to right.** Make a green circle for go and a red circle for stop.
  Left to---------------Right
  ● --------------------- ●
  Go   Stop
- **Children may get distracted when viewing too many words on a page**. Create a reading window by taking a plain bookmark (without any pictures) and cut a small rectangle in the middle just large enough to fit one sentence.

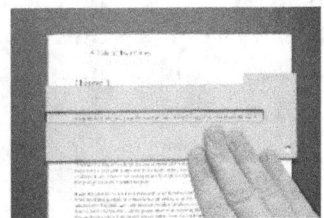

- **Play a game.** Name a body part and ask your child to think of all the words that have the same sound. This game will help build phonics skills.

- **Have your child pretend that he is the illustrator as you read.** That means he should have vivid pictures of the reading in his head.
- **Help your child learn how to pronounce word fragments.** These word fragments can create 500 new words: -ack-ail-ain-ake-ale-ame-an-ank-ap-ash-at-ate-aw-ay-eat-ell-est-ice-ick-ide-ight-ill-in-ine-ing-ink-ip-it-ock-oke-op-ore-ot-uck-ug-ump-unk.
- **Pick the right book.** Make sure you pick a book on your child's reading level for reading aloud activities, it is important that they understand what they're reading.
- **Try choral reading.** You and your child can read aloud at the same time.
- **Peak your child's interest.** Many children find books based on a movie or familiar TV show the most fun to read.
- **Try recorded books.** These materials, available from many libraries, can stimulate interest in traditional reading and can be used to reinforce and complement reading lessons.
- **Helpful strategy for dyslexic children.** Have your child scribble gibberish line by line from left to right to reinforce reading from left to right.
- **Practice, practice, practice.** Remember reading can be done anywhere; a menu, street sign, directions, grocery store items, etc.
- **Use the pictures as cues during reading.** This will help put the reading into context.
- **Compliment your child's strategy.** If your child needs correction say something like, "The word is mouse, but your guessing mice makes sense. Good job with sounding out the words."
- **Use cliff notes.** If your child is struggling with reading the chapters, supplement the book with cliff notes that can be found online or at your local bookstore.
- **Tips for reading textbooks.** Point out titles and any boldfaced subheadings. These headings let your child know what the main topics and main ideas will be.

READING COMPREHENSION

- **Make it interactive.** Have your child pick a color to highlight details before you start reading.
- **Help your child find the main idea.** The main idea of the paragraph is usually found in the first and last sentence.
- **Learn how to focus on the reading.** Your child can mouth or whisper each word to help them focus on the reading.
- **Color code details.** Pick a different color for; vocabulary, definitions, and important facts.
- **Help your child put events in order.** Use a dry erase board to draw a storyboard like a comic strip; it doesn't matter if you have to draw stick figures. You can also create a flow chart drawing arrows from one event to the next. This is also helpful for studying, especially for social studies exams.
- **Try a riddle or mystery.** Find fun riddles online. Riddles stimulate inferential reading comprehension. Go to your local library for a 2-minute mystery book. These books help your child read for content and pick out important details.
- **You may have to repeat reading.** Have your child scan silently first before reading aloud. Read a story over and over again especially if they are struggling with it. That is why it is important to choose something they enjoy.
- **Ask questions after every paragraph.** Read a paragraph and ask your child to summarize it in their own words.
- **Practice reading comprehension at the movies.** After watching a movie, ask your child to summarize everything that happened.
- **Add some emotion when reading.** Show your child how to read with gusto or emotion. This can help them to focus on the reading.
- **Make predictions or "bets."** Constantly ask the child what they think might happen next. Example: "The girl in the story seems pretty brave—I bet she's going to try to save her family."

Comprehension Steps

1. Predict: Use clues from the text or illustrations to predict what will happen next.

2. Questions: Use the question words; who, what, where, when, why, how, and what if.

3. Clarify: Read on. Ask, does this make sense?

4. Summarize: Tell the main ideas of the text in order.

COMMON PREFIXES AND SUFFIXES

It is important to teach your child prefixes and suffixes to help him/her become a more fluent reader and easily understand the meaning words. *Focus on prefixes first because it is easier to teach.

Prefix	Meaning	Examples
bi-	two	bicycle, binoculars
dis-	not	disagree, disappear
ex-	out of	exit, expel
in-	into	inside
mis-	wrong	misspell, mistake
pre-	before	prefix, precede
post-	after	postwar
re-	again	reread, rewrite
re-	back	return, retreat
sub-	under	submarine, subway
super-	above	superman, superior
trans-	across	transportation
tri-	three	tricycle, triangle
un-	not	unhappy, untrue

Suffix	Examples
-al	removal
-ance	clearance
-ence	absence
-ity	stupidity, curiosity
-ment	excitement
-ness	fairness, craziness
-sion	division, explosion
-tion	multiplication
-ant	servant, giant
-ent	student, president
-er	farmer, teacher
-ess	waitress, actress
-ist	artist, cartoonist
-or	actor, sailor
-en	strengthen
-ly	sadly, truly

2 WRITING

HANDWRITING

- **For a child who likes to draw.** If your child likes drawing tell them to write out a word (spelling or vocabulary) as neatly as possible then try to turn the word into a picture. This is a fun way to practice handwriting and spelling.
- **Purchase the right writing supplies.** Felt tip pens glide across the page and help with cursive. Make writing fun by allowing your child to pick out writing utensils that they like. Ex. Your child can choose a pen that is their favorite color. A form fitted pencil holder can greatly improve handwriting. Raised lined paper can help with letter placement because the child will be able to physically feel each line on the paper.
- **Make writing fun.** Start by giving your child short interesting things to write; a postcard to friends/relatives, invitations, or descriptions a favorite TV show. Have a conversation or play a guessing game but the conversation can only be done in writing.
- **Work on technique.** Talk out writing letters, for example when explaining the letter B you can say: 1) Start at the top 2) Straight line down 3) Back to the top 4) Sideways Smile. Sideways Smile. Teach your child writing in ways that they will easily understand. Your child should not hold the pencil too tightly; a grip is too tight if you can't easily pull the pencil out of the hand. Push your child to slow down and take their time. Don't worry handwriting comes together in 4th grade.
- **Remember your child's interests.** For any assignment remember to relate it to their interest. For example, if your

- child loves cats then all homework sentences can be written about cats.
- **Remember which direction to write the letters, "b" and "d".** Write "b" and "d" on your child's hand with a washable marker like the diagram below.

- **Help with Spacing.** Encourage your child to use a pinky finger to specify spacing. Graph paper is useful when writing numbers to keep everything aligned. You can also turn a sheet of notebook paperwork sideways to show how much space should be between each letter.
- **Remember the three S's of handwriting:** Is the letter the right **Size**? Is the letter the right **Shape**? Is there enough **Space** between letters and words?
- **How to correct handwriting.** If you notice sloppy or illegible handwriting, you can ask , "Is that an A or H." Then ask your child to fix it or show him/her how.
- **Use a diagram to help with placement.** Draw a diagram like Charlie the stick figure below. Tell your child the capital A starts at Charlie's foot, comes all the way up to Charlie's head, and crosses at Charlie's belt.

WRITING TIPS: HW SENTENCES AND ESSAYS

- **First pick a topic.** Then brainstorm anything and everything related to that topic. Don't worry about writing neatly or

- writing in complete sentences, you just want your child to get the ideas on paper first. A dry erase board can be very helpful for brainstorming.
- **Choose a topic that is relevant to your child.** Family memories, humorous incidents, scary moments, milestones, likes/dislikes, and things that just happened; are all easy topics to write about.
- **Remember the PLEASE method for writing.** *Pick* a topic, *list* your ideas about the topic, *evaluate* your list, *activate* the paragraph with a topic sentence, *supply* supporting sentences, and *end* with a concluding sentence.
- **Find out all the requirements for a writing assignment.** For example, it may need a title page, table of contents, pictures, or a list of sources.

WRITING AN ESSAY

Planning. The first paragraph needs to grab the reader's attention. It introduces everything that will be discussed. Use a strong thesis (statement you will be proving) to spell out key points. A strong thesis should inspire the reader to ask, "How?" or "Why?"

Sample thesis: Lebron James' ability to score, pass, and rebound make him the league's most valuable player.

Specific topic **+** Attitude/Angle/Argument **=** Thesis

What you plan to argue + How you plan to argue it = Thesis

Writing Your Draft. Jot down everything you can think of related to the thesis and put together any relevant research. Then start placing the information in paragraphs. At the beginning of each paragraph, pull in your reader, and then add additional details in another four to ten sentences. A conclusion reviews key points, creatively restates the thesis, and finishes with an inventive final statement. In other words, give your audience something to think about.

Editing. Make sure your paper flows from sentence to sentence and makes sense. Does this paragraph flow logically from the previous paragraph? Does it support your thesis? Let your thesis be your guide and stay on topic. Replace simple vocabulary with stronger vocabulary words.

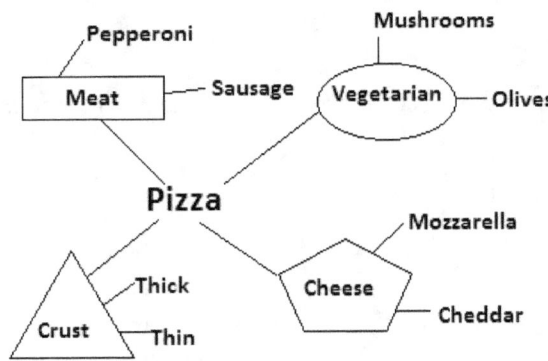

Graphic Organizer:

1) Start with an essay topic

2) Branch out paragraph topics

3) Branch out paragraph topics to details

WRITING COMPLEX SENTENCES

Teach your child the mnemonic, "FANBOYS" to remember words to add to the end of a sentence. Use these words to make simple sentences into complex sentences. It is helpful to have this sheet in front of your child when completing a homework assignment.

Words to Remember (FANBOYS):

- for
- and
- nor
- but
- or
- yet
- so

Starting a Sentence(time):

- earlier
- next
- before
- later
- today
- first
- second
- lastly

Connecting a Sentence

- also
- still
- therefore
- instead
- meanwhile
- however
- then
- rather

Starting a Sentence(make a point):

- of course
- clearly
- definitely
- importantly
- certainly
- in fact
- naturally
- it seems

3 SPELLING

SPELLING TIPS

- **Practice words in a fun way.** Have your child use his finger to spell the word in the air. Your can use an Etch a Sketch or magnetic letters to spell out words.
- **Color-code the patterns in spelling words.** For example, in the words "rough", "tough", and "enough" make the "ough" red.
- **Create a spelling rainbow.** Type or write the spelling words in big letters. Have the child trace over letters of word with a different colored pencil 3 times to create a rainbow.
- **Play a game.** Give each letter of the alphabet a value and have your child find the value of the word. For example, the letter "a" is worth one point, "b" is worth 2, and so forth. Play a game of hangman. Scrabble and boggle are great games to help practice spelling. Play hangman to help your child guess the word.
- **Use a dry erase board.** Write the spelling word really big on the board and break it down into parts.
- **Pronounce each word.** Enunciate each word very slowly so your child can hear every letter sound.

SPELLING STUDY SCHEDULE

Monday
- Pretest on the whole list and put a check next to words that need more practice. Start practicing the first 5 words that were misspelled.

Tuesday-Thursday
- Test on the entire word list. Start practicing the next 5 words that were misspelled.

Friday
- Send your child off with these words: "We practiced all week and we know you're prepared. Do the best you can today, and however you do is fine with me."

4 MATH

MATH TIPS

- **Highlight important information.** Your child may make mistakes by quickly overlooking important information. Teach them how to highlight operational symbols and directions at the top of paper.
- **Remember this mnemonic for long division.** Does McDonalds Sell Burgers? or Dead Monsters Smell Badly-divide, multiply, subtract, and bring down.
- **Make math visual.** Use pictures, drawings, pies, and money to bring the numbers to life. For example, you can cut up a paper circle to explain fractions or draw a clock on the board to practice telling the time.
- **Tips for solving a math problem.** Leave lots of space between math problems to eliminate confusion and distraction. Write the steps out for each problem so your child can follow it step by step.
- **Make word problems more interesting.** Replace the characters in the word problem with characters from TV like Harry Potter or Hannah Montana to make it more relevant.
- **Help for teaching the metric system.** Think of tangible items, such as a liter of soda or a yardstick to help your child visualize measurement.
- **It's never too early to teach your child multiplication.** Learning multiplication facts can be very time consuming. It is important to teach your child early. That way, the teacher will be reinforcing what you have already taught your child.
- **What if I don't know how to solve the problem?** There is usually an explanation of how to solve the problems in the

- beginning of each chapter in the textbook. You can also find sample problems online through a quick google search.
- **Don't be afraid to mark up the textbook.** Get a pencil with a good eraser; underline or write notes next to the problem.
- **Preparing for a math test.** Work out the problems dealing with each topic and don't move onto another topic until there is total confidence that your child can complete it on a test.

HOW TO COMPLETE A MATH WORD PROBLEM

- <u>Start</u> by reading the problem silently to get a general understanding of it.
- <u>Identify and underline</u> all numbers written as digits or words. Look for "hidden numbers."
  (dozen, half as many, see below for more clue words)
- <u>Read</u> the problem aloud. Draw a picture or diagram of it.
- <u>Read</u> the problem again to find out what it is asking for. Underline the question.
- <u>Inquire,</u> "What do I have to do to answer the problem?" (subtract , divide, multiply, etc)
- <u>Give</u> the problem smaller numbers than the one's actually used to make the problem less intimidating.
- <u>Take</u> a pencil and solve the problems and check your answers.

ACE THAT MATH TEST

For each topic that you need to study, complete the ACE steps:

Answer each problem by working it out in writing. It doesn't count until the problem has been solved without looking at the answer, notes, or textbook. Try more challenging problems that the teacher may cover on the test.

Confirm that each answer is correct after working out the problem. If it is not, try the problem again.

Examine your child's understanding of each problem after you have confirmed that the answer is correct. Do this by answering these questions: What was the point of the problem? What common errors does my child need to avoid when working out a problem like that?

DECODING WORD PROBLEMS

Use these tables to help your child figure out what keywords mean.

Words for Addition

Add	Additional	All	Altogether	Both	Combined	In all
Increased by	More than	Sum	Plus	Raise	Together	Total

Words for Subtraction

Changed	Decreased by	Difference	Dropped	Exceeded	Fewer
Have left	Less than	Lost	More	Reduced	Remain
Subtract	Take away	Are not			

Words for Multiplication

At	Multiply	Of	Times	Twice	Double	Triple

Words for Division

Cut	Each	Every	Out of	Split	Shared	Quotient

5 FOCUS STRATEGIES

FOCUS TIPS

- **Say the right thing.** Don't say: "Finish your homework, then study spelling, and then do your book report. Say: "Let's work to complete the problems on this page in the next 10 minutes." It is important not to overwhelm your child with too many tasks all at once.
- **Use repetition.** Ask your child to repeat what you instructed, if the child is defiant about repeating then this technique shouldn't be used. You should also repeat information until your child pays attention to what you say. Be patient even if you feel you sound like a broken record.
- **The best time for consequences.** Our recommendation is to make a request, wait 15 seconds, issue a warning, and then provide a consequence within 5 additional seconds if the child does not follow through.
- **Don't hover during homework time.** You should be close enough to provide necessary help but you don't always need to hover over them.
- **Hide the timer.** A timer can be used if you feel your child is taking too long to complete a task. However, if you use a timer, keep the timer out of view to minimize distraction.
- **Power down electronics.** All electronics including cell phones should be turned off during homework time.
- **Create a comfortable environment.** Lighting and temperature play a big role in keeping your child focused.
- **Eliminate distracting items.** If the child picks up an item during the session take it out of their hand immediately.
-

- **Create a study space at home.** If the computer is distracting, choose a space away from it. The child should only have necessary items on the table.
- **Show your child how to relax.** Tell your child to imagine that they are in a movie theatre. Then picture the lights in the theater dimming and then tell your child to keep focusing on the screen. Then imagine the screen slowly fading to black. Teach children that when their bodies are relaxed, they are better able to think and plan.
- **Be very patient.** Allow your child to have enough time to think, never be quick to give the answer. It may take 15 minutes of repeating the question and allowing your child to have time to think for them to get the correct answer.
- **Keep it interesting.** Maybe your child is not paying attention because they need more stimulation, so try to incorporate other games and activities.
- **Keep a checklist of tasks.** Your child will be calmer if they know what to expect.
- **Choose the right time and place for your child to do homework.** Maybe your child works best right after school or maybe they need a short break. Choose the best time that works for your child.
- **Make sure your child is not hungry.** Allow your child to have a healthy snack before starting homework. A hungry child is a distracted child
- **Use a pointer.** A bright colored pencil can help your child follow along as you read. You can also push your child to use a finger to follow along as you read.
- **Set up a homework schedule.** There should be structure, routine, and most importantly consistency.
- **Use eye contact.** If you your child is not paying attention remind them to look at you when you talk by making eye contact.
- **Teach your child how to pay attention.** You can say, "you look like you're paying attention when…"

- **Remind your child that homework is almost completed.** You can say, "We only have 3 more problems to do then we will be finished."
- **If your child doesn't want to sit down, take a break.** Don't say anything, take a deep breath and then say, "I let you have a break now it is time to finish up the homework."
- **Let your child read the instructions.** Have your child read the instructions for homework. This pushes your child to pay attention to what the question is asking.

6 SCHOOL STRATEGIES

ADJUSTMENTS

- **Handwriting frustrations.** Ask the teacher to allow your child to write in print rather than cursive if they are struggling with handwriting.
- **If your child always forgets the textbooks.** Borrow another set of books for home use.
- **Your child should be an active learner.** Simply asking a few questions or contributing to class discussions will let teachers know that they are paying attention. Class participation can also help boost grades.
- **Eliminate school distractions.** It is important to speak with your child about his classroom environment to make sure that it is comfortable. Something as small as a wobbly chair can be highly distracting.
- **Use your school's resources.** There are many resources available at each school such as after school programs or a reading specialist.
- **Always be polite to school staff.** By being polite and cooperative when working with the school, you will also avoid being perceived as an intrusive parent. Teachers respond most positively to parents who aren't looking to blame them for their children's struggles.
- **Ask the teacher for homework accommodations.** Ask the teacher if you can write homework assignments for your child. That does not mean you will be completing the homework, it will just make them feel less intimidated to complete the task. This simple change has been really beneficial for many children.
- **Classroom Adjustments.** Sit the student with good role models. Ask the teacher to give your child more time for tasks.

Establishing frequent eye contact, and placing the student in the front row near the teacher's desk, can also help. Students should be asked to put away unnecessary items, and a work area should be provided away from distractions. Limit in-class reading, send some reading assignments home.

- **Communication is important.** Your child may mention something about what the teacher does and then you can go back to the teacher and figure something out that works. Talk with your child about issues at school and solutions to fix them.
- **Remind the teacher that your child needs breaks.** Allowing your child to hand out papers can be a great way to release energy. Generally, ADHD students do better when given extra classroom structure, and shorter work periods. Your child can go to the bathroom or do an errand for the teacher to blow off some energy.
- **Communicate with his teacher frequently.** Get a communications book where you can write back and forth to the teacher or use weekly progress report to keep track of your child's performance in the classroom. Even if your child is performing well it is important to schedule conferences throughout the year to make sure your child continues working well at school.
- **Have a back up plan for homework.** Know whom to call if your child is missing homework.
- **Children should have a sense of teachers as humans, not merely authorities.** When your child thinks, "She's strict, but she's cool," what she means is, "We can work together."

THE PERFECT CLASSROOM FOR AN ADHD CHILD

- Structured and positive
- Engaging instruction materials
- Clear expectations and predictable schedules
- Clearly defined and enforced rules and consequences
- Structured work environment, tasks, and materials
- Assistance through transitions such as from recess to back to the classroom

- Discreet cuing and reminders
- Learning style accommodations
- Extra time for tasks
- Creative and interesting lesson plans
- Choices, options, and flexibility such as selecting 5 questions to complete rather than the entire worksheet
- Feeling they have a choice in decision making
- Ongoing support and coaching in areas that are weak
- Help coping with feelings of frustration
- Teamwork between school personnel, parents, and health providers

7 ORGANIZATION

TIME MANAGEMENT AND ORGANIZATION

- **If your child is struggling with keeping track of assignments.** Ask the teacher to check the homework assignment book and initial if the assignments are written down correctly.
- **Lighten the backpack.** Keep minimal notebooks, binders, texts, and extra papers in the backpack.
- **Use a monthly calendar.** Use a monthly calendar to keep track of future assignments.
- **Encourage your child to get into the habit of putting away all books.** All notebooks, assignments, and folders should be inside his backpack before bedtime.
- **Keep a pen in the ring of the planner.** Your child will be more likely to use the planner if they do not have to search through the bag every time something needs to written down.
- **Keep your planner accessible.** The best place to keep a planner is on the desk to make it more accessible.
- **Your child should write down his assignments A.S.A.P.** Your child shouldn't wait until the end of the day when they will be more likely to forget the assignment.
- **Keep a smaller binder.** A small binder will force your child to clean it out and organize it more regularly.
- **You have to get organized so your child can get organized.** Use a bulletin board for any loose papers or reminders.

- **Fill a bucket with homework supplies.** That way you can easily move it If you need to move to a computer.
- **Use one folder.** If your child can't keep track of separate folders, start off with one folder.
- **Keep an organized locker.** Label the spines of books to help your child find their books easier especially when they need to take them home.
- **Keep an organized backpack.** Papers shouldn't be stuffed into the backpack. Your child should at least slide it into the front of pocket of his binder or a folder. They should prepare everything the night before to avoid searching for papers in the morning.
- **Help with executive functioning.** Create a visual chart of chores that shows the sequence of morning to evening activities. As your child completes the task, move the clothes pin down next to the corresponding picture.
- **For a child who doesn't want a planner.** You don't have to buy a traditional planner. For example, a wallet filled with post it notes can be great for reminders. Think of a creative way to help your child keep track of assignments.
- **Create a checklist.** Make a checklist by drawing pictures instead of words for tasks that need to be completed.
- **Speak with your child about organization.** Give your child reasons why getting organized is about making life easier not harder. After the first major cleanup done with your assistance, start each evening study session with a five minute "tidy-time." Eventually your child will form the habit of his own.
- **Be creative.** Do what works for your child, maybe just a spiral notebook will work but make sure you have a stapler to staple any papers inside.
- **Brain dump the to-do list.** Spend 10-15 minutes jotting down all the to do list items: 1) Start each item with a verb, don't use the word decide. 2) Apply the 3 minute rule, if it can be completed in less than 3 minutes, just get it out the way now. 3) Transfer items to the planner's calendar. 4) Now create an action list of how to get these things done.

- **Know where everything is.** Have a consistent place to keep everything. Gather everything needed for a homework assignment, such as a dictionary or calculator.
- **Use a separate folder.** If your child won't bring home the handouts, decorate a separate folder just for handouts and reward your child with a sticker each time it is brought home.
- **Purchase three clear pocket-type folders.** Label the pockets "Homework to do," "Homework done," and "Notices." Clear folders allow your child to immediately see what contents are inside the folder.

ASSIGNMENT SHEET

If your child does not like carrying a planner, you can use a homework sheet for each week. Make sure it becomes a routine. You can say, "Just like you take your pencil out for each class, you assignment sheet should always be on your desk so you can write down your assignments." This can be stored in a folder or the front pocket of a binder.

Sample:

Week of: _____

Subject	Monday	Tuesday	Wednesday	Thursday	Friday	Weekend
Math						
Science						
English						
History						
Art						
Other						

HOW TO TAKE NOTES

Complete Sentence Notes:

To summarize what someone says:

-Shorten what is said or read.

-Write only key points

-Have them retell stories to you. Ask questions.

-Cross off unnecessary words

Outline Notes:

I. Title

  1. Subject

    a. Item 1: Description

    b. Item 2: Description

    c. Item 3: ....

  2. Subject 2

II. Title 2

ESTIMATE THE TIME TO COMPLETE A TASK

List tasks in order of importance. Although math does not have to be the first item on the list, it should be high enough that your child is sure to get to it. Allot more time than you think is needed to make sure that there is enough time to complete the task.

Sample list:

Sunday	*Hours*	*Monday*	*Hours*
Math	1	History	2
English	2	Science	1
Clean Room	1	Math	1
Totals	4		4

8 TEST PREPARATION

TRUE AND FALSE TESTS

If your child is stumped these are general test taking tips that may be helpful. Remember these rules do not always apply.

Statements Most Likely to be True:

- The most general statement
- The most complete statements
- All of the above choice
- The longest choice
- If two choices are opposite, choose one of them

Statements Most Likely to be False:

- If alternatives range in value, eliminate the two extremes
- Humorous statements
- Absolute statements e.g. all, always, everybody, none, etc.

STUDY TIPS

- **Find out what your child already knows.** Ask your child to tell you anything he knows about the subject. This will help you relate the information to what he already knows rather than studying from scratch. Instead of drilling in new information it is better to start with what your child already knows. You can ask, "Tell me everything you know about this vocabulary word in your own words." If your child does not know anything then ask him to read the definition. After your child reads, then
-

you can explain it in a way that he would remember. (See Mnemonics and Strategies for Improving Memory)

- **Studying for a vocabulary test.** 1) Go over all the words and have your child repeat the definition after you. 2) Now ask your child, to give you the meaning in their own words. 3) Go over vocabulary words that your child finds challenging. 4) Play a game or create a fill-in-the-blank test

- **Reminders for taking the test.** Read the question first so your child knows what to look for. Stress that he/she needs to read all the directions on a test. When he/she receives a test, it is helpful to immediately write down any information that was memorized, such as formulas or specific dates, because that information is harder to remember.

- **Make studying fun.** Play crazy eights but before laying down a card, your child has to call out the answer to a question. Play tic tac toe. Your child is x and you're o, ask your child a question and if he answers correctly mark x if not you mark o. If your child loves sports; draw a football, soccer, or baseball field where they can earn goals for each question. Instead of a board use a yardstick and with each correct answer your child can move their clothespin an inch up. They win if they reach the end of the yardstick.

- **Prepare study materials.** Draw pictures for a study sheet instead of writing down the information. Use stick figures if you are not good at drawing.

- **For fill in the blank questions.** Write the answer choices that might fit above the blanks then pick the one that fits best.

- **Preparing for the test.** 1) Know the schedule for the tests beforehand and create a study schedule. Make sure your child has actually studied in increments and not crammed before the test. 2) Encourage your child to study actively by marking up his papers and notes with underlines or highlights. 3) Have your child make up questions that might be on the test or go over the review questions in the back of the chapter. 4) Go over the questions the teacher says will be on the test. 5) Make sure your child is well rested and fed, if the time allows you can treat your child to breakfast.

- **Remember the STAR method.** 1) **S**urvey the test to see which items can be answered quickly. 2) **T**ake time to read the directions carefully. 3) **A**nswer the questions that can be answered quickly, leaving difficult items for last. 4) **R**eread the questions and answers, making any needed corrections.

- **Look at old tests.** Analyze any errors so you know what mistakes your child is making, maybe they are just forgetting to read the directions properly. For example, your child may be mixing up synonyms and antonyms. File the tests for cumulative exams in the future.

- **Use flashcards.** Instead of saying, "I'll make flashcards for you." Say, " This is how you make yourself a set of flashcards." This will push your child to learn how to create his own study materials. Write the word and definition on the front of the notecard. Then have the child cut the card in half and match the pieces together.

- **Aim for a 100% when studying for a test.** Tell your child, "The higher the grade you aim for on the test the higher the grade you are likely to get." This mindset pushes your child to study *all* possible topics not just ones they think is on the test.

9 MEMORY

MEMORY TIPS

- **Make the information meaningful.** Repeating words without connecting them to a meaning is like trying to hang your clothes in the closet without hangers. Relate the material to your child's interests. You can also relate the information to a child in the class or a friend.
- **Be creative.** Scented markers or scented stickers stimulate memory on a test. You can use different scented markers to write different information.
- **Make it memorable.** Say the information in a weird voice. Replace words in a song with the new information such as "old MacDonald had a farm, aeiou." Your child can teach you how to do the homework assignment, teaching new information to others helps with memory.
- **Exercise your child's memory.** When your child is losing interest, you can play this game: tell him to stare at a vase (or other detailed object). Then tell your child to close their eyes, imagine it, and tell you about it with details.
- **Start with memorization.** Memorizing or reviewing information should be done at the beginning when both you and your child are fresh.
- **Learn how to create mnemonics.** Here are some examples: When two **c**ars **c**ollide they make a dent-accident. There is definitely no A in definite. Everyone **love**s a **love**ly present. If you use two **C's** and two **E's** you will su**ccee**d. For the word parallel imagine the 2 l's in the word being parallel. To **a**ffect something **a**lters it, but the **e**ffect is the **e**nd result. Use eat, an apple, as, a, nice, snack to remember the continents: Europe,

Asia, Africa, Australia, Antarctica, North America, and South America.

- **Explore memory techniques.** Does your child form pictures in their mind when reading? Encourage them to build whatever works.
- **Show your child how to be an active learner and use different senses.** For new information, your child should be able to **hear it, see it, say it, and do it**.
- **Repetition.** Your child should read the information and repeat it after you say it.

10 TEACHING STRATEGIES

HOW TO BE A CONNECTED PARENT

The more you keep your child engaged-about anything no matter how big or small- the more your child will discuss her difficulties with homework. Remember that listening leads to connection. To encourage further talking say phrases such as, "Tell me more," "Go on," "How do you feel about that?" and "I know what you mean," or "Then what?" Instead of butting in with your advice or opinion, listen for and name the feelings you think you hear, based on what your child is telling you. "Sounds like that made you pretty mad, didn't it?" or "You seem really happy about that!" Also, use problem-solving phrases when needed. "What do you wish you could do?" or "What do you want to happen?" or "What do you think will happen if you do that?"

Distracted children are more motivated to do classwork and homework for teachers they feel connected to. You may have to empathize with your child's negative thoughts about homework to get to the bottom of the real problem. By empathizing, you are not agreeing with or condoning homework. Rather, you are removing communication barriers that block the ability to discuss the homework issues.

Overreactions can emotionally overwhelm your child, causing your child to have less motivation. Overreacting does not make you a bad parent. However, if you frequently overreact, not only will it prevent you from effectively using the strategies; it can actually worsen the problem.

HOW TO APPROACH HOMEWORK

- **Brain dump for a project.** Write down everything your child knows and color code which ideas go together.
- **Compare your child's passion to homework success.** For a child who plays sports, you can say: "How many times do you practice catching, making baskets or throwing the ball. Well, we're going to do the same with punctuation."
- **Make a statement:** Don't say: "Do you want to start homework now?" or "Would you do me a favor and get out your homework book?" Do say: "Please begin your assignment now."
- **Set Goals.** Don't set your child up to fail by setting goals that are very difficult to achieve especially in the beginning. Start with a goal your child is almost guaranteed to achieve to build confidence. For example, he will complete x amount of problems in x time with x amount correct.
- **Mean what you say and say what you mean.** Be patient with your child's response because your child may test you in the beginning. Your child won't believe you unless you are consistent. Your child may initially not like your reassertion of authority. Make clear how many times you are going to repeat instruction before negative consequences.
- **Using Punishment.** Use a 4:1 reward to punishment ratio to avoid discouragement, anger, and aggressiveness.
- **Be specific.** If you hear, "don't think of a pink elephant." The first thing you start thinking of is a pink elephant. Say what child is supposed to be doing not what they should not do. "You are supposed to begin working now." Not "Stop daydreaming and wasting time." Emphasize that you want your child to do their "best work" on HW not their "fastest work."
- **Be positive.** When reviewing homework, start with what has been completed correctly before revisions. Don't give backhanded compliments E.x.: "This is a really neat and organized math HW page. You really are improving. Maybe next time you'll get the answers right." Instead say a sincere

- reinforcing compliment, "Look you've even got more answers right than last time."
- **Use this chart to get an idea of how long an assignment should take.** To get an average of how much homework your child should be getting: multiply 10 minutes by their grade level.
- **Be encouraging.** The child whose performance is low doesn't need reminding; your child needs encouragement and reassurance that you value them regardless of performance.
- **Try a different approach.** Be humorous and share jokes, homework doesn't have to be totally serious
- **Children who have ADHD tend to be "concrete" thinkers.** They often like to hold, touch, or take part in an experience in order to learn something new. By using games and objects to demonstrate mathematical concepts, you can show your child that math can be meaningful and fun.
- **If your child says they can't do it, act as if they can.** Ask what parts do you understand? What parts are you getting stuck on?
- **Make sure your child is not overwhelmed.** What other activities does your child have going on? Is it interfering with homework?
- **Make it interesting.** Writing on yellow paper with black ink stimulates learning. Get your child a computer game for learning. Be willing to move on to something else.
- **Reduce writing.** Allow your child to respond to homework questions orally.
- **Ask questions.** Ask your child questions about the material to determine their understanding. If your child asks you a question about homework, don't just give a straight answer, explain why or ask them a question.
- **ADHD children generally do not transition well.** Give your child "lead time." For example, rather than saying "8:00 p.m. -- bedtime," it works better if you give some lead time by saying, "Bedtime in 15 minutes…bedtime in 10 minutes…bedtime in 5 minutes."

REWARD SYSTEMS

- **Introduce the token system to your child:** Present it in a positive light, such as, "We are going to begin using a system to reward you for all the efforts you are putting in at homework time." Have all the materials for the program in front of you to show your child. The child will be given tokens for their accomplishments or good behavior, which can be eventually traded in for rewards.

- **Discuss the token system with your child.** Create a plan that incorporates small rewards for small victories and larger rewards for bigger accomplishments. Reward examples: (worth more tokens) bringing home assignment book, (worth less tokens) sharpening pencils for homework. Parents should follow the rules of the points system and not be too generous. Younger children like tokens and older children tend to like points.

- **Use the system to keep your child on task.** If your child is losing focus, remind them of the reward. Remember that as much as your time is valuable, it is just as valuable for your child. You can say, "After we finish this, you will have the rest of the evening to play."

- **Rewarding isn't bribing.** Few adults would show up to work without getting paid. You don't have to buy a reward. Reward him with things that build your relationship with each other. You can say, "If we finish this, you and mom can make cookies together." If your child wants to play a favorite game, you can say, "After you can show dad how to beat that round in the game." If it is a material reward, you can gradually phase it out when it is no longer needed.

- **Involve the child in the process of setting the house rules and setting the consequences for breaking them.** A child who feels included in setting the rules will be more likely to respect them.

- **Create a reward menu.** Say, "We are going to start a program in which you can earn things. Let's start a list." If your child names an expensive item or time-consuming activity, you can

- direct the child to cut a picture of the item out of a magazine or draw a picture of it. The picture can be cut into smaller pieces. Each time the child earns a reward; a part of the picture can be pasted onto a piece of paper on the refrigerator. When the picture is completed, the reward is earned.

- **Know when to give a reward.** Children with ADHD respond best to specific goals and daily positive reinforcement—as well as worthwhile rewards. Giving concrete rewards every time your child is productive is not always practical. Tokens can be a practical way to implement the rewards system. Some parents keep tokens in their pockets at all times so that positive behaviors can be reinforced immediately.

- **Praise your child.** Praise should focus on the positive action; give praise immediately, the sooner the approval is given the more likely the student will be to repeat it. Vary praise so it doesn't lose its value.

- **Use mystery rewards to make the system more appealing to your child.** Reward systems can become stale, so mix it up. The name of a reward can be written on a piece of paper and placed in an envelope labeled, "mystery reward." Alternatively there can be a grab bag of small items, such as those purchased at a dollar store. Create a spinning wheel, dartboard, or roll a die, with the child receiving a reward that corresponds with the number that is obtained on the spinner, board, or die. Your child should know that bonuses are always available for exceptionally good behavior.

- **What is Positive Reinforcement?** Providing a consequence that makes a behavior more likely to happen again. If you did not receive a paycheck for going to work and doing your job, you would probably stop going to that job. Furthermore, if your boss is someone who lets you know when you are doing a good job, you are more likely to want to work hard for that person.

- **"I don't agree with the reward system."** Sometimes parents do not feel particularly comfortable giving out rewards.

    A) "I should not have to reward my child for things she should already be doing." We agree: Your child should already be acting appropriately at home. *Reality check: Start where your child is, not where you think your child should be.*

B) "I'll go broke!" Rewarding your child does not always mean buying something new. In fact some of the most valuable rewards are those that you don't have to pay for.
C) "My child will expect something every time he behaves well." *First things first:* The immediate goal is to improve your child's behavior and performance. Over time you may find that you can reduce how frequently you give rewards. However, when you start provide rewards more frequently.
D) "There is no reward that will work for my child." Perhaps you need to try mystery rewards to peak your child's interest. Be creative, and discuss with your child what he or she may like to earn.
E) "This all takes too much time." It is important to you that your child is more productive so it is necessary to put in some time to help your child. However, as it becomes routine, less time will be required.
F) "My child feels nothing is rewarding." Be creative, ask other parents, or attend a local CHADD meeting.

- **Don't criticize your child's ideas for rewards.** Some children will volunteer expensive items, which are inappropriate for daily rewards. Do not criticize you child's ideas. Some of them can be placed on a menu called long-term rewards. Then provide examples of short-term rewards such as a special dessert, 30 minutes of television, or video game time.
- **Don't give a child a reward if he hasn't earned it.** If a child doesn't deserve a reward this time. Don't criticize; just express your hope that he or she will receive a reward next time.
- **Attention can be a reward.** Parents often say, "My child misbehaves to get attention." This shows you how even attention can be a reward for a child. The key is to only give the child positive attention such as praise to reward good behavior.
- **Why specificity is important.** Rewarding a child for "being good" can be very confusing and does not let the child know what he or she has done to be reinforced. Instead of saying

"you earned a reward for being good," you can say, "you earned reward for following directions without any reminders."

- **Make sure the reward is meaningful.** Make sure you continue to change reward systems because what may be meaningful this month may not be meaningful to your child next month.

TYPES OF INTELLIGENCE

Tap into your child's learning style to determine the best way to help them with schoolwork.

Word smart (linguistic intelligence): These children like words and how they are used in reading, writing, or speaking. This child may enjoy word play and word games, storytelling, reading, or creative writing.

Music smart (musical intelligence): These children appreciate music, rhythm, melody, and patterns in sounds. They are capable of hearing tone and pitch. This child enjoys singing, playing instruments, and listening to music. Tape record information or replace the lyrics of popular songs with information that your child needs to study.

Logic Smart (logical-mathematical intelligence): This child enjoys figuring things out and may understand numbers and math concepts, like finding patterns, and have fun with science. These children may enjoy brainteasers, computers, creating their own codes, or doing science experiments.

Picture smart (spatial intelligence): These children love to look at the world and see all the interesting things in it. This child can picture images in his head. He may use his imagination to show others his vision through art, design, photography, architecture, or invention. Use charts, maps, notes, and flashcards. Practice visualizing or picturing words/concepts in your head. Write out everything and draw pictures for quick visual review.

Body smart (bodily-kinesthetic intelligence): This child is graceful and comfortable using their body to learn new skills or express themselves in different ways. This child may be an athlete or dancer. Or may have an interest in working with her hands doing crafts, building models, or repairing things. Facts that must be learned should be written several times. Trace words as you are saying them. Make study sheets.

People smart (interpersonal intelligence): These children are interested in other people and how people interact with each other. This child may be a part of student government, have lots of friends, or just enjoy being in casual social groups. Study groups may be helpful for this child.

Self smart (intrapersonal intelligence): This child is aware of and understands their feelings, what they're good at, and the areas they wants to improve. These children may keep a journal. Create plans for the future and help this child set goals for themself.

Nature smart (naturalist intelligence): This child enjoys identifying and classifying things like plants, animals, or rocks. These children may be interested in gardening, cooking, or taking care of pets. Make connections to their interests when studying.

A Note to Parents

Is it realistic to hope that this book will help turn your child into a homework lover? Probably not. Homework resistance may never completely disappear. However, your child's struggles will be much more manageable if you consistently apply the techniques in the book. Consistency will make all the difference. If you are not consistent then your child will not be able to get the complete support and guidance that they need. Consistency is so important that I would recommend every parent to stick the word "Consistency" in big bold letters on the refrigerator as a daily reminder. Try to stay patient and realize that progress usually comes for those parents and children who stick with it.

SOURCES AND RESOURCES

Power, Thomas J. *Homework Success for Children with ADHD*. The Guilford Press, 2001.

Fender, Gloria. *Learning to Learn: Strengthening Study Skills and Brain Power*. Incentive Publications, 2004.

Rief, Sandra F. *The ADHD Book of Lists*. Jossey-Bass, 2003.

Kutscher, Martin. *Organizing the Disorganized Child*. Harper Paperbacks, 2005.

Woodcock, Susan Kruger. *Soar study skills*. Grand Lighthouse, 2006.

Honos-Webb, Lara. *The Gift of ADHD: How to Transform Your Child's Problems Into Strengths*. New Harbinger Publications, 2005.

Clark, Faith. *Hassle Free Homework*. Main Street Books, 1989.

Gold, Mimi. *Help for the Struggling Student*. Jossey-Bass, 2003.

Iseman, Jaqueline. *101 School Success Tools for Students with ADHD*. Prufrock Press, 2010.

Parker, Harvey. *Problem Solver Guide for Students with ADHD: Ready-to-Use Interventions for Elementary and Secondary Students*. Specialty Press, 2001.

Moss, Samantha. *Where's My Stuff?: The Ultimate Teen Organizing Guide*. Orange Avenue Publishing, 2007.

Hunt, Jan. *ADHD-Modifications for School Success: A Guide for Teachers, Parents and Students Kindergarten through College*. Cambridge Cottage Press, 1998.

Graham, Steven. *Writing Better: Effective Strategies for Teaching Students With Learning Difficulties*. Brookes Publishing Company, 2005.

Schumm, Jeanne Shay. *How to Help Your Child with Homework: The Complete Guide to Encouraging Good Study Habits and Ending the Homework Wars.* Free Spirit Publishing,2005.

Stevens, Chris. *Thirty Days Has September: Cool Ways to Remember Stuff.* Scholastic Nonfiction,2008.

Packer, Leslie. *Challenging Kids, Challenging Teachers.* Woodbine House, 2010

Lockett, Sharon Marshall. *Home Sweet Homework: A Parents Guide to Stress-Free Homework & Studying Strategies That Work.* Adams Media,2007.

Jacobelli, Frank. *ADD/ADHD Drug Free: Natural Alternatives and Practical Exercises to Help Your Child Focus.* AMACON,2008.

Smith, Richard Manning. *Mastering Mathematics: How to Be a Great Math Student.* Brooks Cole,1999.

Bernstein, Jeffrey. *10 days to a Less Distracted Child: The Breakthrough Program that Gets Your Kids to Listen, Learn, Focus and Behave.* Da capo Press, 2007.

ABOUT THE AUTHOR

Sharlene Alexander, developed a passion for children at an early age. During her freshman year of high school, she tutored her neighbor's son who was diagnosed with dyslexia and ADHD. After working with him, she received several referrals and continued tutoring ADHD students throughout college. She found that her techniques were successful and saw a great need for a program that helped ADHD students. After graduating Binghamton University, she decided to start Mommy Alert. Mommy Alert provides parents of ADHD children with invaluable resources and strategies.